United States Government Accountability Office

Report to the Chairman, Committee on Small Business, House of Representatives

I0448836

July 2013

EXPORT PROMOTION

Better Information Needed about Federal Resources

GAO-13-644

EXPORT PROMOTION

Better Information Needed about Federal Resources

GAO Highlights

Highlights of GAO-13-644, a report to the Chairman, Committee on Small Business, House of Representatives

Why GAO Did This Study

In 2010, the President launched the NEI with the goal of doubling U.S. exports over 5 years. More than 2 decades ago, Congress directed the President to establish the TPCC to provide a unifying framework for federal efforts in this area. Among other things, Congress directed the TPCC to assess the appropriate levels and allocations of resources and develop a government-wide strategic plan that identifies federal export promotion priorities, reviews current programs in light of these priorities, and proposes to the President a federal trade promotion budget that supports the plan. Congress also required the TPCC to submit annual reports to Congress describing the required strategic plan.

This report assesses the extent to which the TPCC compiles and reports information on how federal export promotion resources are aligned with export promotion priorities. GAO reviewed the laws governing the TPCC and good practices for interagency initiatives, analyzed TPCC budget data and documents, and interviewed TPCC secretariat and Office of Management and Budget staff.

What GAO Recommends

GAO recommends that TPCC (1) develop and distribute guidance for member agencies on what information they should provide the TPCC on the resources they spend on export promotion activities; and (2) report in its National Export Strategies on how resources are allocated by agency and aligned with the strategy's priorities. The TPCC secretariat agreed with our recommendations and stated it plans to take steps to address them.

View GAO-13-644. For more information, contact Kimberly Gianopoulos at (202) 512-8612 or gianopoulosk@gao.gov.

What GAO Found

The interagency Trade Promotion Coordinating Committee (TPCC) neither reports nor compiles information on how federal export promotion resources align with government-wide priorities. As a result, decision makers lack a clear understanding of the total resources dedicated across the country and around the world by TPCC member agencies to priority areas, such as increasing exports by small- and medium-sized businesses. GAO has previously reported that effective national strategies should address costs and has found shortcomings in the committee's response to the budget-related portions of its mandate. While the TPCC's National Export Strategy reports issued since initiation of the National Export Initiative (NEI) outline government-wide priorities and progress in achieving them, they do not discuss how resources are allocated in support of these priorities. Despite the current emphasis on export promotion as a high-priority goal, recent strategies have provided less information on budget resources than have previous strategies, as shown below. The TPCC last publicly reported a summary budget table in 2008. TPCC secretariat officials acknowledged that the TPCC agencies currently place little emphasis on displaying or discussing agencies' resources in the National Export Strategy.

National Export Strategy Presentation of Budget Information

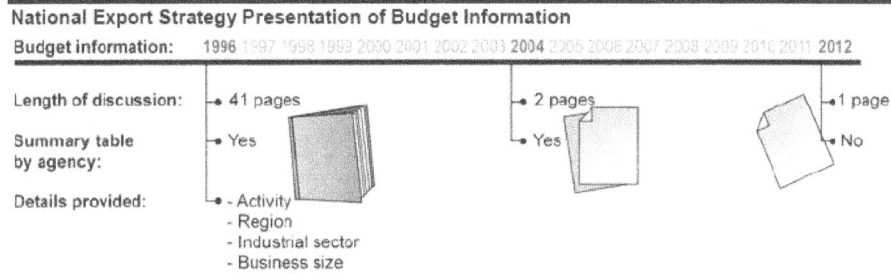

Source: GAO analysis of Trade Promotion Coordinating Committee information.

The TPCC last compiled high-level data on member agencies' budget authority in 2011, but this information is not useful for assessing resource allocations. To be useful, data should, among other things, be consistent and sufficiently complete for the intended purpose. However, the TPCC's data are inconsistent across agencies and not detailed enough to facilitate an understanding or comparison of how resources are allocated among priorities. TPCC agencies do not use a common definition of export promotion, so it is unclear why some agencies are included in the TPCC's data and others are not, and the TPCC's data are not current. Although agency accounting systems and budget processes differ, which presents challenges, clear guidance for agencies on what information they should provide the TPCC could improve the quality of the data. Without better information on agencies' export promotion resources, decision makers cannot determine whether the federal investment in export promotion is being used effectively or make informed decisions about future resource decisions.

Contents

Abbreviations

Ex-Im	Export-Import Bank of the United States
GPRA	Government Performance and Results Act of 1993
NEI	National Export Initiative
OMB	Office of Management and Budget
ONDCP	Office of National Drug Control Policy
OPIC	Overseas Private Investment Corporation
SBA	Small Business Administration
TPCC	Trade Promotion Coordinating Committee
USAID	United States Agency for International Development
USTDA	United States Trade and Development Agency
USTR	United States Trade Representative

GAO

U.S. GOVERNMENT ACCOUNTABILITY OFFICE

441 G St. N.W.
Washington, DC 20548

July 17, 2013

The Honorable Sam Graves
Chairman
Committee on Small Business
House of Representatives

Dear Mr. Chairman:

In January 2010, the President launched the National Export Initiative (NEI) with the goal of doubling U.S. exports over 5 years. In doing so, the President drew renewed attention to a long-standing challenge: effectively coordinating the many and varied federal programs aimed at supporting growth in U.S. exports. More than 2 decades ago, Congress directed the President to establish the interagency Trade Promotion Coordinating Committee (TPCC) to provide a unifying framework for federal export promotion and export financing programs.[1] Under the Export Enhancement Act of 1992, Congress directed the TPCC to assess the appropriate levels and allocations of resources for export promotion and export financing efforts.[2] The law further required theTPCC to develop a government-wide strategic plan and provide annual reports to Congress describing the plan and its implementation.[3] These strategic plans are to identify priorities, review current export promotion programs in light of these priorities, and propose to the President a federal trade promotion budget that supports the TPCC's plan for priority activities and improved coordination and eliminates funding for identified areas of overlap and duplication.

You requested that we review information about federal export promotion resources available to TPCC agencies. This report assesses the extent to which the TPCC currently compiles and reports information on how federal export promotion resources are aligned with established priorities.

---

[1]Export Enhancement Act of 1992, Pub. L. No. 102-429, § 201, 106 Stat. 2186. codified as amended at 15 U.S.C. § 4727.

[2]Id.

[3]15 U.S.C. § 4727.

GAO-13-644 Export Promotion

To address this objective, we analyzed the laws and presidential directives that define what is required of the TPCC as an interagency coordinating body, including the budget-related requirements in the Export Enhancement Act of 1992. We also reviewed GAO's guidance regarding data reliability and examined good practices for coordinating interagency initiatives, as described in other GAO reports, including those covering the Government Performance and Results Act (GPRA) of 1993 and the GPRA Modernization Act of 2010. We reviewed budget data collected by the TPCC, the TPCC's annual National Export Strategies (focusing in particular on reports issued since the NEI was announced), and other TPCC documents describing efforts to compile and report budget information. We also interviewed TPCC secretariat and Office of Management and Budget (OMB) staff. For more details about our objectives, scope, and methodology, see appendix I.

We conducted this performance audit from February 2013 to July 2013 in accordance with generally accepted government auditing standards. Those standards require that we plan and perform the audit to obtain sufficient, appropriate evidence to provide a reasonable basis for our findings and conclusions based on our audit objectives. We believe that the evidence obtained provides a reasonable basis for our findings and conclusions based on our audit objectives.

Background

Responsibility for designing and carrying out federal export promotion programs is widely dispersed. Numerous federal agencies have offices across the country and overseas and operate a wide variety of programs that are intended, at least in part, to assist U.S. companies in entering foreign markets or expanding their presence abroad. For example, agencies provide companies with information on market opportunities and help them connect with potential buyers abroad, provide access to export financing, and negotiate with other countries to lower trade barriers.

The dispersion of export promotion activities among numerous agencies led us to observe in a 1992 report that "funding for ... agencies involved in export promotion is not made on the basis of an explicit government-wide strategy or set of priorities. Without an overall rationale it is unclear whether export promotion resources are being channeled into areas with the greatest potential return."[4] In 1992, Congress passed the Export Enhancement Act of 1992, which directed the President to establish the TPCC.[5] The TPCC is chaired by the Secretary of Commerce, and its day-to-day operations are carried out by a secretariat that is housed in Commerce's International Trade Administration. The TPCC has 20 members, including 7 core members.[6] Oversight of these agencies is dispersed across many congressional committees. Table 1 identifies the authorizing and appropriating subcommittees with jurisdiction over the seven core TPCC agencies.

Table 1: Congressional Committees with Jurisdiction over Core TPCC Agencies

	Subcommittees under Committees on Appropriations		Authorizing committees with jurisdiction	
Agency	House	Senate	House	Senate
Commerce (International Trade Administration)	Commerce, Justice, Science and Related Agencies	Commerce, Justice, Science, and Related Agencies	Foreign Affairs	Banking, Housing, and Urban Affairs Commerce, Science, and Transportation
Ex-Im	State, Foreign Operations, and Related Agencies	State, Foreign Operations, and Related Agencies	Financial Services	Banking, Housing, and Urban Affairs
OPIC	State, Foreign Operations, and Related Agencies	State, Foreign Operations, and Related Agencies	Foreign Affairs	Foreign Relations
SBA	Financial Services and General Government	Financial Services and General Government	Small Business	Small Business and Entrepreneurship

[4]GAO *Export Promotion: Federal Programs Lack Organizational and Funding Cohesiveness,* GAO/NSIAD-92-49 (Washington, D.C.: Jan.10, 1992).

[5]Pub. L. No. 102-429, § 201.

[6]TPCC members as specified in the Export Enhancement Act of 1992 are the Departments of Commerce, State, the Treasury, Agriculture, Energy, and Transportation; the Agency for International Development (USAID); the Trade and Development Agency (USTDA); the Small Business Administration (SBA); the Overseas Private Investment Corporation (OPIC); the Export-Import Bank of the United States (Ex-Im); and the Office of the U.S. Trade Representative, as well as other departments or agencies as the President determines necessary. In Executive Order 12870, the President added the Departments of Defense, Labor, and the Interior; the Environmental Protection Agency; the Council of Economic Advisors; the Office of Management and Budget; the National Economic Council; and the National Security Council. 58 Fed. Reg. 190 (Sept. 30, 1993). The seven core members are the Departments of Commerce, State, and Agriculture; USTDA; SBA; OPIC; and Ex-Im.

| | Subcommittees under Committees on Appropriations | | Authorizing committees with jurisdiction | |
Agency	House	Senate	House	Senate
State	State, Foreign Operations, and Related Agencies	State, Foreign Operations, and Related Agencies	Foreign Affairs	Foreign Relations
USDA (Foreign Agricultural Service)	Agriculture, Rural Development, Food and Drug Administration, and Related Agencies	Agriculture, Rural Development, Food and Drug Administration, and Related Agencies	Agriculture	Agriculture, Nutrition, and Forestry
USTDA	State, Foreign Operations, and Related Agencies	State, Foreign Operations, and Related Agencies	Foreign Affairs	Foreign Relations

Source: GAO.

We have reviewed the TPCC's operations on several occasions since its creation in 1992.[7] We have found that the TPCC and its member agencies have improved coordination in several areas, but we also found shortcomings in the committee's response to the budget-related portions of its mandate. In 2002, we observed that the Secretary of Commerce, as the chair of the TPCC, made recommendations to the President, through OMB, on selected export promotion budget matters on multiple occasions. However, with no authority to reallocate resources among member agencies and occasional agency resistance to its guidance, the TPCC provided limited direction over the use of export promotion resources in support of its strategies. We also noted that the TPCC had not used its National Export Strategies to examine how agencies' resources aligned with their goals, and we recommended that the TPCC consistently do so. The TPCC agreed with our findings and recommendation. However, in 2006 we determined that the committee had not implemented our recommendation; we found that the committee's annual strategies did not review agencies' allocation of resources in relation to identified priorities. In 2009, we observed that the TPCC's most recently published National Export Strategy continued to lack an overall review of agency resource allocations relative to government-wide priorities.

Export promotion has recently been emphasized as a high priority for the federal government. In his 2010 Executive Order announcing the NEI, the

---

[7]For a list of GAO reports on the TPCC and related topics, see the Related GAO Products section at the end of this report.

President emphasized that creating jobs and sustainable economic growth in the United States was his top priority, and that increasing exports was a critical component of those efforts. He also laid out eight priority areas to be addressed through the NEI.[8] OMB subsequently identified the NEI's goal of doubling U.S. exports as one of 14 interim crosscutting priority goals under the GPRA Modernization Act.[9] Additionally, as part of his 2013 and 2014 budget proposals, the President proposed consolidating six departments and agencies involved in export promotion into one new cabinet-level department.[10]

In his directives regarding the NEI, the President established a new body, the Export Promotion Cabinet, to develop and implement the initiative.[11] The Export Promotion Cabinet is coordinated by a White House official, has most of the same member agencies as the TPCC, and is to coordinate its efforts with the TPCC. Among other things, the President tasked the Export Promotion Cabinet to work with the TPCC to determine how resources should be allocated. In particular, a February 2012 Presidential Memorandum instructed the Export Promotion Cabinet, in consultation with the TPCC, to evaluate the current allocation of federal government resources, make recommendations to the Director of OMB for their more effective allocation, and propose a unified federal trade budget, consistent with the administration's priorities, to the Director of OMB as part of the annual process for developing the President's budget.

---

[8]The NEI's priority areas are (1) exports by small- and medium-sized enterprises; (2) federal export assistance; (3) trade missions; (4) commercial advocacy; (5) increasing export credit; (6) macroeconomic rebalancing; (7) reducing barriers to trade; and (8) export promotion of services.

[9]This act calls upon OMB to develop long-term, outcome-oriented goals for a limited number of cross-cutting policy areas, and to provide information on how they will be achieved. Parts of the act do not come into effect until the 2015 budget is issued, but the act requires OMB to develop interim goals starting with the 2013 budget. Pub. L. No. 111-352, 124 Stat. 3866 (2011) (amending the Government Performance and Results Act of 1993, Pub. L. No. 103-62, 107 Stat. 285 (1993)). For comments on each of the interim crosscutting priority goals provided in the President's budget, see GAO, *Managing for Results: GAO's Work Related to the Interim Crosscutting Priority Goals under the GPRA Modernization Act,* GAO-12-620R (Washington, D.C.: May 31, 2012).

[10]The President proposed consolidating into a single department the Department of Commerce's core business and trade functions: SBA, USTR, Ex-Im, OPIC, and USTDA. The proposal would also incorporate related programs from a number of other departments.

[11]Exec. Order No. 13534, 75 Fed. Reg. 12433 (Mar. 11, 2010).

The TPCC Does Not Report or Collect Information on How Resources Align with Priorities

National Export Strategies Outline Priorities, but Do Not Identify Associated Resources

The Export Enhancement Act states that the TPCC's strategies should establish a set of priorities for federal export promotion activities and propose a unified federal trade promotion budget that supports the plan.[12] Additionally, we have previously reported that one of the six characteristics of an effective interagency national strategy is that it identifies the resources needed to carry out the strategy. Specifically, an effective national strategy should address what it will cost, the sources and types of resources and investments needed, and where resources and investments should be targeted based on balancing risk reductions with costs.[13]

The most recent National Export Strategies, published in 2011 and 2012, outline federal priorities for export promotion, but provide little information on member agencies' resources for carrying out these priorities. Both strategies outline progress made toward the eight NEI priorities and identify specific areas federal agencies will focus on in the coming year. In fact, the 2011 strategy includes the NEI recommendation to "increase the budget for trade promotion infrastructure" as one of five critical recommendations on which TPCC agencies would focus. However, these strategies do not provide summary information on the total resources available for export promotion and do not discuss how resources are currently allocated across priorities. Without this information, decision makers lack a clear understanding of the total federal resources being dedicated to export promotion activities, and it is not possible to assess the appropriate levels or allocations of export promotion resources.

---

[12]15 U.S.C. § 4727(c).

[13]GAO, *Combating Terrorism: Evaluation of Selected Characteristics in National Strategies Related to Terrorism,* GAO-04-408T (Washington, D.C.: Feb. 3, 2004).

The 2011 and 2012 strategies contain very limited discussions on agencies' export promotion resources, consisting only of a few bullets that broadly discuss agencies' budget requests. For example, figure 1 reproduces in its entirety the section in the 2012 report titled "The Administration's FY2013 Trade Promotion Budget." The section includes three bullets relating to agencies' requested export promotion budgets for 2013, but provides no context on the total federal export promotion budget or on the budgets of the individual agencies it discusses. The first bullet, for example, notes that the President's budget proposed $30.3 million in additional funding for the U.S. and Foreign Commercial Service's overseas export promotion activities. However, it does not indicate what the Commercial Service's baseline budget is, whether the increase supports specific priorities laid out in the strategy, or whether resources could be shifted from existing Commerce activities, or from other agencies, to meet these needs. The remaining bullet points do not tie specific funding requests to individual agencies. The second bullet states that the fiscal year 2013 President's budget seeks "support" for SBA's Office of International Trade without stating what amount of funding, if any, SBA is requesting. The final bullet point simply states that five other core TPCC agencies seek a total increase of $19 million over 2012 funding levels.

Figure 1: 2012 National Export Strategy Discussion of the Export Promotion Budget

The Administration's FY 2013 Trade Promotion Budget

The Federal Government is improving performance and making progress toward accomplishing NEI objectives with existing resources. However, as competition for new global middle-class consumers, major infrastructure projects, and inward investments intensifies, support for achieving the NEI's goals for U.S. exports and the jobs they support calls for new resources in some discrete areas.

The President's FY 2013 budget seeks the following:

- Department of Commerce: $30.3 million to expand the U.S. and Foreign Commercial Service's overseas export promotion activities and $12.3 million to implement the SelectUSA program of promoting business investment in the United States by foreign and domestic sources.

- SBA: Support for SBA's Office of International Trade to leverage SBA's business loan programs to finance exports. SBA's export finance and counseling were greatly enhanced by the passage of the Small Business Jobs Act, which increased the maximum size of export loan guarantees and expanded SBA's network of export finance specialists.

- Other core TPCC agencies: an increase of $19 million over 2012 levels for the Ex-Im Bank, U.S. Trade and Development Agency, USTR, the U.S. International Trade Commission, and the Overseas Private Investment Corporation.

Source: Trade Promotion Coordinating Committee, 2012 National Export Strategy

Despite the current emphasis on export promotion as a high-priority goal, the level of detail on agencies' budgets presented in the TPCC's National Export Strategies has decreased. During much of the 1990s, the TPCC provided trade promotion budget information by agency and by activity, noting as it did so that presenting meaningful information across agencies was difficult because of the variety of programs involved. The strategies provided in-depth tables on how agency resources were allocated, for example, the 1997 report included 44 pages of material on this topic. After 2000, the TPCC stopped reporting budget information in such depth. The National Export Strategies from 2002 through 2008 provided only a summary budget table that presented information on each agency's total budget authority for export promotion activities. As already noted, the most recent reports have eliminated these summary budget tables. Figure 2 compares the budget information presented by the TPCC in 1996, 2004, and 2012.

Figure 2: Major Changes in National Export Strategy Presentation of Budget Information

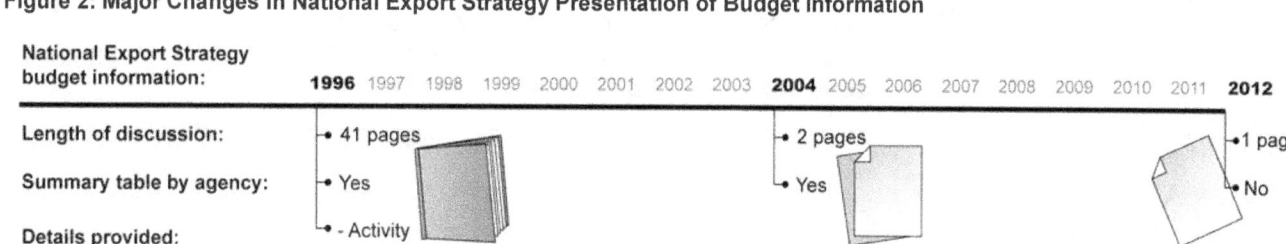

National Export Strategy budget information:

1996 1997 1998 1999 2000 2001 2002 2003 **2004** 2005 2006 2007 2008 2009 2010 2011 **2012**

Length of discussion: 41 pages | 2 pages | 1 page

Summary table by agency: Yes | Yes | No

Details provided:
- Activity
- Region
- Industrial sector
- Business size

Source: GAO analysis of Trade Promotion Coordinating Committee information.

TPCC secretariat officials acknowledged that the amount of budget information presented in the National Export Strategies has declined and that the TPCC members currently place little emphasis on displaying or discussing agencies' resources. They noted that changes in the political and budget environment over time have affected the TPCC's processes. First, TPCC secretariat officials said that in the early 2000s, the TPCC shifted its focus away from resources in favor of efforts to improve the management of existing programs. For example, in 2003, a TPCC secretariat memo to member agencies stated that, given the budget environment, agencies should assume their budgets would be flat. The TPCC recommended that agencies look for opportunities to leverage resources through coordination or by sharing costs. Because the TPCC anticipated that members' appropriations would not be increasing, secretariat officials stated that the TPCC largely stopped talking about or examining resources. Officials further noted that, while the NEI has generated enthusiasm for export promotion, the TPCC's current focus remains on better managing and coordinating existing resources.[14] Second, TPCC secretariat officials also stated that because final appropriations have not been passed until later in the fiscal year, it has been more difficult to collect up-to-date budget data. Finally, though GPRA sought to improve agency management and reporting processes, TPCC secretariat officials indicated that, as member agencies increasingly worked to comply with the law in 1999, it hindered their ability

---

[14]TPCC secretariat officials stated that they try to influence agencies to use discretionary funding in support of TPCC priorities, but it is difficult to make recommendations about the allocation of resources, in part because the TPCC is chaired by the Secretary of Commerce, one of its many member agencies, who has no specific authority over other agencies.

GAO-13-644 Export Promotion

to do crosscutting analyses. Officials found that agencies focused on their own specific core priorities and on developing agency-specific performance plans, which complicated the TPCC's ability to obtain and track export promotion budgets.

The Budget Data the TPCC Collects Are Not Useful for Assessing Resource Allocations

The TPCC Collects Some High-Level Budget Data

The TPCC periodically collects summary data on agencies' total budget authority for export promotion activities with OMB's assistance. According to OMB staff, OMB asks agencies' budget offices to self-identify their activities that relate to export promotion and compile a summary budget number. OMB resource management offices typically review the numbers provided by the agencies to ensure they are reasonable. Table 2 below reproduces the last table publicly released by the TPCC in its 2008 National Export Strategy, including its footnotes.

Table 2: TPCC Data on Select Member Agencies' Export Promotion Budget Authority, Fiscal Years 2007 to 2009

Dollars in millions

Agency	FY 2007 Actual	FY 2008 Enacted	FY 2009 Request
Department of Agriculture	674	644	563
Department of Commerce	356	339	350
Department of State[a]	176	184	198
Department of Treasury	3	3	3
Export-Import Bank	38	1	3
Overseas Private Investment Corporation[b]	(192)	(165)	(170)
Small Business Administration	5.2	6	6.4
Trade and Development Agency	50	51	51
U.S. Trade Representative	44	44	46
Total	**1,346**	**1,272**	**1,220**

Source: TPCC.

Notes:

This table reproduces the data presented in the TPCC's 2008 National Export Strategy in its entirety.

Note to original TPCC table: "Amounts may be restated in the future to reflect new data or definitions. Figures may include administrative expenses, transfers, or other adjustments."

[a]Note to original TPCC table: "Dollars are cumulative of all business and economic activities in the State Department."

[b]Note to original TPCC table: "Totals do not include OPIC."

According to OMB staff, OMB only compiles this information when requested by the TPCC, and the committee last requested this data in the spring of 2011. Because the TPCC opted not to make these data public in that year's National Export Strategy, OMB staff did not fully review them. Therefore, OMB staff requested that we not publish the data collected in 2011. We nevertheless examined the more recent information the TPCC provided us, which included actual budget data for the same member agencies as shown in table 2 from fiscal years 1994 through 2010 and agencies' requested budget for fiscal years 2011 and 2012. The TPCC used the same process to collect data in 2011 that it used for the 2008 National Export Strategy. Therefore, our discussion below, which identifies several significant issues impacting the reliability and usefulness of the data, focuses on the 2011 update but also generally applies to the data presented in table 2. According to TPCC secretariat officials, the committee has initiated efforts to further update this information, but officials have not indicated whether they plan to make it public as part of a future National Export Strategy.

The TPCC's Data Are Not Consistent or Comprehensive Enough to Understand How Resources Are Allocated

The data the TPCC collects are not useful for assessing the allocation of export promotion resources. To be useful for assessing how agencies' resources are allocated, data should, among other things, be consistent and sufficiently comprehensive for the intended purpose.[15] Moreover, collaborating agencies would need to use compatible methods to track funding.[16] Additionally, we have reported on the importance of agencies providing appropriate levels of detail in budgeting documents. For example, prior to the creation of the Department of Homeland Security, we noted that crosscutting funding data provided in an OMB annual report on combating terrorism had limited utility for decision makers, in part because it did not include data on obligations or on duplication in

---

[15]According to GAO's guidance on assessing the reliability of computer-processed data, consistency refers to the need to obtain and use data that are clear and well defined enough to yield similar results and similar analyses. See GAO, *Applied Research and Methods: Assessing the Reliability of Computer-Processed Data*, GAO-09-680G (Washington, D.C.: Feb. 2009).

[16]GAO, *Managing for Results: Key Considerations for Implementing Interagency Collaborative Mechanisms*, GAO-12-1022 (Washington, D.C.: Sept. 27, 2012).

programs for combating terrorism.[17] We identified several issues with the TPCC's most recent data, from 2011, and determined that the data are neither consistent across agencies nor comprehensive enough to indicate how resources are allocated across priorities or the overall cost of carrying out the National Export Strategy.

- **Agencies use different definitions:** According to TPCC secretariat and OMB staff, each agency independently defines export promotion and self-identifies the activities to include in its export promotion budget. The TPCC's data include few explanatory notes about how each agency's budget was computed, making it difficult to compare numbers across agencies or understand what activities are included for each agency. In fact, TPCC secretariat officials were not always certain what each agency's number represented. Because agencies use different definitions, there is no assurance that TPCC's data treat similar activities consistently. For example, SBA, OPIC, and Ex-Im all provide some form of export financing, but the TPCC's data for these agencies represent three different aspects of their budgets. SBA's data show the administrative expenses for its Office of International Trade, which is responsible for its export loan programs. OPIC's data capture the agency's total impact on the federal budget but do not provide any indication of the costs of operating its financing programs. Ex-Im's data show the appropriations for its Office of Inspector General, but do not include any information on the costs of operating its financing programs or the agency's total impact on the federal budget.[18]

- **The reasons for including or excluding agencies are not always clear:** An example of the lack of clarity in how the TPCC treats member agencies is that its summary budget table does not include USAID, noting that it does not do so because the agency's activities

---

[17]GAO, *Combating Terrorism: Funding Data Reported to Congress Should Be Improved*, GAO-03-170 (Washington, D.C.: Nov. 26, 2002). See also GAO, *Veterans' Health Care Budget: Better Labeling of Services and More Detailed Information Could Improve the Congressional Budget Justification*, GAO-12-908 (Washington, D.C.: Sept. 18, 2012), in which we pointed out that more detailed information could improve the Department of Veterans Affairs Congressional Budget Justification.

[18]This only applies to Ex-Im submissions provided after fiscal year 2008. Since fiscal year 2008, Ex-Im has been self-sustaining for appropriations purposes, financing its operations from receipts collected from its borrowers. Therefore, Ex-Im's budget submissions prior to 2008 used a different formulation than those submitted after 2008.

GAO-13-644 Export Promotion

support trade promotion indirectly. However, the TPCC's data include OPIC, which also focuses on international development and only indirectly supports exports. Moreover, the TPCC's table continues to include other agencies, such as the Department of the Treasury, which do not directly fund trade promotion activities. Nonetheless, as we noted in 2006,[19] portions of several National Export Strategies continued to highlight export promotion programs involving USAID.[20] According to TPCC secretariat officials, member agencies decide whether or not they have export promotion programs and whether to provide resource data.

- **The data are not detailed enough to align with priorities:** The TPCC's summary budget table presents data at a very high level, with one number for each agency, and provides no information on specific activities or programs. Without greater detail, it is not possible to understand whether or how agency resources are aligned with the priorities laid out in the National Export Strategy and National Export Initiative. Some TPCC member agencies conduct activities in more than one priority area. For example, among other activities, Commerce supports U.S. business in conducting trade missions and also works to reduce barriers to trade, both of which are priority areas in the National Export Initiative. Among its many activities, USDA supports the goals of increasing exports by small and medium-sized enterprises and increasing export credit available to U.S. businesses. Because it only presents information at a high level, the TPCC's table does not allow users to understand how federal resources are being allocated across these, or other, priority areas.

- **The data are not current:** The TPCC's data are not comprehensive because they do not include current information about agencies' resources. The TPCC last updated its information in April 2011 and that summary budget table reflected agency budget requests for fiscal year 2012. The President released his fiscal year 2013 budget request in February 2012. Nonetheless, the latest data collected by

---

[19]GAO, *Export Promotion: Trade Promotion Coordinating Committee's Role Remains Limited*, GAO-06-660T (Washington, D.C.: Apr. 26, 2006).

[20]For example, the 2012 National Export Strategy includes a discussion of a 4-year, $120 million USAID program, the African Competitiveness and Trade Expansion Initiative, which provides funding for African Regional Trade Hubs. The strategy notes that these hubs promote increased trade between sub-Saharan African countries and the United States. The cost of this program, however, is not captured in the TPCC's budget data.

the TPCC do not reflect fiscal year 2013 requests, nor do they show actual data for 2011, or estimates for 2012. Moreover, because the TPCC opted not to include the data in its National Export Strategy, OMB staff never fully vetted the data collected in 2011. Therefore, the most recent fully vetted data on federal export promotion resources are from 2008.

- **Budget authority data does not fully reflect costs of all agencies' programs:** Finally, the TPCC's use of total budget authority data provides an incomplete picture of the costs of some agencies' programs. For example, OPIC is self-funded through receipts collected on its financing activities and has a net negative budget authority, meaning it returns money to the U.S. government. However, it does receive annual instructions from Congress on the amount of money it can spend on administrative and program expenses for its financing programs. While the TPCC's use of total budget authority data may accurately represent one aspect of an agency's impact on the overall federal budget allocated for export promotion, it is not sufficiently detailed to fully understand the agency's contributions toward export promotion. For example, the TPCC's number does not indicate the costs associated with operating OPIC's financing programs or how much financing its budget supports.

Without consistent and comprehensive information on export promotion resources, the TPCC cannot accurately assess the levels and allocation of resources among agencies. Thus, decision makers in Congress and the administration do not have full information about the U.S. government's investment in export promotion and cannot determine whether resources are being allocated to the highest priority areas. Further, without information on export promotion resources, neither the TPCC nor the Export Promotion Cabinet can make informed recommendations about their appropriate allocation across agencies. Additionally, the Export Enhancement Act requires the TPCC to identify overlap and duplication among export promotion programs. However, as we have reported, it is difficult to gauge the magnitude of the federal commitment to a particular area of activity or assess the extent to which federal programs are duplicative without a clear understanding of the costs of implementing those programs and the activities they support.[21]

Lack of Clear Guidance Impedes the Collection of Useful Data

According to TPCC secretariat officials, the TPCC does not provide any guidance to agency officials on what budget information should be reported or how agencies should determine which activities should be included as export promotion. In the past, the TPCC provided guidance on the information member agencies should submit on their export promotion budgets. We reported that the data presented by the TPCC fostered a better understanding of historic and potential expenditures.[22]

The lack of clear TPCC guidance makes it difficult for agencies to provide, and for the committee to collect, comparable budget information. Without clear guidance, TPCC agencies use different definitions for export promotion in compiling budget information. Many agencies' programs have multiple objectives, some of which are directly related to export promotion and some of which are not. For example, USDA's export promotion programs also fulfill domestic agricultural objectives. According to OMB staff, this makes it challenging to clearly determine what activities should be considered export promotion. OMB staff stated that TPCC secretariat and OMB staff have had some preliminary discussions about developing standardized definitions of what activities should be considered export promotion and how data should be reported. However, these discussions are in the early stages, and the TPCC would need to decide what information it wants to include in the National Export Strategies before moving forward.

Similarly, the TPCC does not supply guidance that could help clarify what level of detail agencies should provide to them. As the TPCC noted in its 2000 National Export Strategy, its ability to collect and present detailed budget information is limited by agencies' abilities to generate comparable data within their varied accounting structures. In developing guidance, the TPCC could work with member agencies to determine a reasonable level of detail and identify the limitations of the data. For

---

[21]GAO, *2013 Annual Report: Actions Needed to Reduce Fragmentation, Overlap, and Duplication and Achieve Other Financial Benefits*, GAO-13-279SP (Washington, D.C.: Apr. 9, 2013).

[22]GAO, *National Export Strategy*, GAO/NSIAD-96-132R (Washington, D.C.: Mar. 26, 1996).

example, in 2000, the TPCC provided details on agencies' expenditures in major federal export promotion areas, such as combating foreign export subsidies. However, they included a caveat that detailed budget numbers below the overall agency total can be difficult to validate and should only be used as an indication of the resources available for each area.

There are lessons to be learned from other bodies coordinating crosscutting government programs and facing similar challenges.[23] For example, like the TPCC, the Office of National Drug Control Policy (ONDCP) has a statutory requirement to develop a national strategy and propose a consolidated budget to implement that strategy.[24] ONDCP's process for developing the National Drug Control Strategy and its associated budget is not a perfect comparison for the TPCC because ONDCP has different authorities for reviewing and suggesting changes to member agencies' budgets. However, its process for collecting and compiling data can highlight the usefulness of providing clear and detailed guidance.[25] ONDCP provides detailed guidance to relevant agencies on how to assemble budget information.[26] Its guidance includes a sample budget table that identifies the level of detail agencies should provide, including a list of the functions, such as corrections or interdiction, agencies should report on.[27] ONDCP's guidance also defines those

---

[23]In addition to ONDCP, discussed above, the Intellectual Property Enforcement Coordinator also has a statutory mandate to coordinate the development of a Joint Strategic Plan which shall include resource estimates. 15 U.S.C. §§ 8111, 8113. In 2010 we reported that the Coordinator had not done so because data collection and analysis were still in progress. See GAO, *Intellectual Property: Agencies Progress in Implementing Recent Legislation, but Enhancements Could Improve Future Plans,* GAO-11-39 (Washington, D.C.: Oct. 13, 2010). We have also recommended that the Director of National Intelligence include a discussion of resources in a strategic framework for its Joint Duty Program, a personnel rotational program across the intelligence community. See GAO, *Intelligence Community Personnel: Strategic Approach and Training Requirements Needed to Guide Joint Duty Program,* GAO-12-679 (Washington, D.C.: June 20, 2012).

[24]21 U.S.C. §§ 1703(b)(2) and 1703(c)(2)(A).

[25]See 21 U.S.C. § 1703(c) for more detail on ONDCP's authorities with respect to the National Drug Control Program budget.

[26]ONDCP Circular: Budget Formulation (Jan. 18, 2013).

[27]ONDCP's use of the term "budget function" does not refer to the major functions of the federal budget. Rather, ONDCP uses "budget function" to describe a particular area of federal involvement.

functions and identifies which activities should be included in each function. In 2011, we reported that, while drug control agency officials raised some concerns about ONDCP's budget process, officials at 4 of 6 agencies stated that it was somewhat or very effective at providing a record of national drug control expenditures, among other things.[28]

Clear guidance can help overcome challenges and make the data collected by interagency groups more useful for understanding how resources are currently allocated across agencies and activities, as illustrated by the ONDCP example. The TPCC's lack of guidance impedes the collection of accurate, comprehensive, and consistent information necessary to understand how resources are allocated among priorities. Without clear guidance, TPCC agencies are using nonstandardized definitions to identify activities that relate to export promotion and are not clear about what level of detail is required.

Conclusion

In announcing the National Export Initiative, the President not only reemphasized the importance of exports to the U.S. economy, but specifically highlighted the need to understand and coordinate federal resources for export promotion. However, the TPCC does not provide decision makers—including Congress and the Export Promotion Cabinet—with information that provides a clear understanding of how resources are currently allocated across the country and around the world among its member agencies or across federal export promotion priorities. In fact, the amount of information the TPCC has reported on agencies' resources has declined. The TPCC has responded to the National Export Initiative by reporting on efforts to address established priorities and working to improve interagency coordination, but the committee currently places almost no emphasis on understanding the federal resources dedicated to implementing the National Export Strategy, as is called for in good practices. In the absence of clear guidance, the data the TPCC collects are not comparable across agencies and not comprehensive enough to allow the TPCC to determine how resources are currently allocated in support of priority activities. Furthermore, without better resource data, neither the TPCC nor the Export Promotion Cabinet can make informed recommendations about how federal resources should be

---

[28]GAO, *Office of National Drug Control Policy: Agencies View the Budget Process as Useful for Identifying Priorities, but Challenges Exist*, GAO-11-261R (Washington, D.C.: May 2, 2011).

allocated. As policymakers review the success of the NEI and consider the President's request for authority to consolidate trade agencies in a single department, it is important to understand how federal resources are being spent. Without consistent and comprehensive information on export promotion resources—presented transparently through the TPCC's annual strategies—decision makers in Congress and the administration cannot determine whether the return on the federal investment in export promotion is adequate or make informed decisions about future resource allocations.

Recommendations for Executive Action

To improve the consistency, comprehensiveness, and transparency of information provided to Congress and policymakers on the federal investment in export promotion programs, the Secretary of Commerce, as chair of the TPCC, should

1. develop and distribute guidance for member agencies on what information they should provide the TPCC on the resources they spend on export promotion activities, and

2. report in its National Export Strategies on how resources are allocated by agency and aligned with priorities.

Agency Comments and Our Evaluation

We provided drafts of this report to the Secretary of Commerce, as chair of the TPCC, and to OMB. In written comments reprinted in appendix II, the Director of the TPCC Secretariat generally concurred with our recommendations on behalf of the Secretary and stated that they intend to work with TPCC member agencies and the Export Promotion Cabinet to implement them. In particular, they plan to create a new TPCC Budget Working Group to establish a robust TPCC role in assessing the appropriate levels and allocation of resources among agencies, as called for in its mandate. TPCC Secretariat officials provided technical comments and suggested corrections and clarifications that we incorporated, when appropriate. Nevertheless, the Director noted the TPCC's limited authority over budget reporting and resource allocations, including its inability to compel member agencies to provide budget and resource information. He gave examples of some challenges they face, including shifts in the political and budgetary landscape and how different Administrations and Congresses have emphasized different priorities over time. However, he said the TPCC Secretariat will work within its existing authorities with TPCC agencies to address our recommendations.

We support the establishment of a TPCC Budget Working Group and note that implementing the requirements of the Export Enhancement Act of 1992 is the responsibility of the committee, as comprised of the member agencies, under the leadership of the Chair and with the support of the secretariat. TPCC member discussions that improve the consistency, comprehensiveness, and transparency of information provided to Congress and policymakers can help overcome such challenges, facilitate well-informed resource decisions, and better support the National Export Initiative and the Export Promotion Cabinet.

We also requested comments on a draft of this report from OMB. On June 21, OMB's Office of General Counsel provided us with comments via e-mail. OMB noted that, while export promotion budgetary data have not been presented in a public document since the 2008 National Export Strategy, OMB annually compiles and reviews current and proposed resources across TPCC agencies that are devoted to export promotion and trade activities, as part of the development of the President's budget. OMB further stated that it uses these data to ensure prudent government-wide allocation of export promotion-related resources and strong support for the President's export promotion agenda, but that because these data are internal, pre-decisional, and deliberative, OMB does not share the cross-agency table outside of OMB, nor does it publish this information as part of the President's budget or related materials. However, OMB commented that it consults with a number of officials, including the Assistant to the President and Deputy National Security Advisor for International Economics, as head of the Export Promotion Cabinet, when recommending export-promotion related resources in the President's budget.

We acknowledge that OMB conducts a review as part of the annual agency budget formulation process. However, this activity is distinct from the TPCC's budget-related requirements in the Export Enhancement Act. As OMB notes, its activities are internal and deliberative and not shared outside OMB, including with the TPCC Secretariat or its member agencies. Thus, OMB's process is not transparent to Congress or to other relevant parties and does not benefit from activities that could improve the consistency or comprehensiveness of this information.

As agreed with your office, unless you publicly announce the contents of this report earlier, we plan no further distribution until 28 days from the report date. At that time, we will send copies to the Secretary of Commerce (in her capacity as Chairman of the TPCC), as well as the

Director of OMB, interested congressional committees, and other interested parties. In addition, the report will be available at no charge on the GAO website at http://www.gao.gov.

If you or your staff have any questions about this report, please contact me at 202-512- 8612 or gianopoulosk@gao.gov. Contact points for our offices of Congressional Relations and Public Affairs may be found on the last page of this report. GAO staff who made major contributions to this report are listed in appendix IV.

Sincerely yours,

Kimberly Gianopoulos,
Acting Director, International Affairs and Trade

Appendix I: Scope and Methodology

This report assesses the extent to which the Trade Promotion Coordinating Committee (TPCC) currently compiles and reports information on how budgetary resources are aligned with established export promotion priorities.

To address this objective, we analyzed the laws and presidential directives that define what is required of the TPCC as an interagency coordinating body. These included the Export Enhancement Act of 1992, which directed the President to establish the TPCC; the 1993 Executive Order which established the TPCC in accordance with the 1992 act; the 2010 Executive Order announcing the National Export Initiative (NEI); and a subsequent (2012) Presidential Memorandum providing further instruction on Export Promotion Cabinet and TPCC collaboration to maximize the effectiveness of Federal trade programs. We also reviewed GAO's guidance regarding data reliability and examined alternate models and good practices for coordinating and managing multi-agency initiatives as described in other GAO reports, including those covering the Government Performance and Results Act (GPRA) of 1993 and the GPRA Modernization Act of 2010. We reviewed the annual "National Export Strategy" reports to Congress that the TPCC has produced since its inception, focusing in particular on those prepared since the NEI was announced in 2010, as well as TPCC memoranda documenting efforts to compile and report budget information and develop a federal trade promotion budget. We also interviewed staff of the TPCC Secretariat, which is housed in the Department of Commerce, and staff of the Office of Management and Budget (OMB).

To assess the reliability and usefulness of budget data collected by the TPCC, we took a number of steps, including (1) reviewing the data for internal consistency; (2) comparing TPCC's data table with select agency budget documents, including Congressional Budget Justifications, appropriations bills, and agency financial or annual reports; (3) reviewing past GAO work on the TPCC's budget; and (4) interviewing knowledgeable TPCC secretariat and OMB staff. Based on this assessment, we identified numerous issues with the TPCC's data, as discussed in detail in this report. We present the TPCC's data in the report only to illustrate our assessment of the data.

We conducted this performance audit from February 2013 to July 2013 in accordance with generally accepted government auditing standards. Those standards require that we plan and perform the audit to obtain sufficient, appropriate evidence to provide a reasonable basis for our findings and conclusions based on our audit objectives. We believe that the evidence obtained provides a reasonable basis for our findings and conclusions based on our audit objectives.

Appendix II: Comments from the Trade Promotion Coordinating Committee

TRADE PROMOTION COORDINATING COMMITTEE

TPCC

Kimberly Gianopoulos
Acting Director, International Affairs and Trade
United States Government Accountability Office
Washington, D.C. 20548

Dear Ms. Gianopoulos:

Thank you for the opportunity to comment on the Government Accountability Office (GAO) draft report <u>Export Promotion: Better Information Needed about Federal Resources</u>: GAO-13-644. We generally concur with the recommendations focused on developing and distributing guidance for member agencies on reporting information to the TPCC and that the TPCC provide more information in the annual National Export Strategies on how resources are allocated by agency and aligned with priorities.

The TPCC Secretariat, within the scope of its authorities and mandate, will work with the Secretary of Commerce as TPCC Chair and with OMB and the TPCC agencies to address these recommendations. However, as agency representatives have noted in exchanges relating to this report and in the context of previous GAO reports and recommendations on this issue, the TPCC Secretariat has limited authority regarding TPCC agencies' budget reporting and resource allocations. Within the limits of these authorities, and with the support of the current Administration and Export Promotion Cabinet, the TPCC Secretariat will work with TPCC agencies to try to address these two specific recommendations.

As a preliminary matter, we note that the draft report does not appear to differentiate between the Secretary of Commerce as TPCC Chair, the TPCC agencies, and the TPCC Secretariat. As the Chair, the agencies, and the Secretariat have different mandates, responsibilities, and authorities, distinguishing these actors would provide for a clearer understanding of this issue.

Regarding the substance of the draft report, we note that the sweeping historical accounting of the TPCC's record on the resource allocation function does not explain or appear to consider the broader context of parallel shifts in the political and budgetary landscape. For example, comments on pages nine and ten on the reduced level of budget reporting starting in 2000 and regarding the 2003 memorandum from the Secretary of Commerce as TPCC Chair (mistakenly attributed to the TPCC Secretariat) recommending a refocusing on leveraging and sharing existing resources do not acknowledge how different Administrations and Congresses have emphasized different priorities. Another example is the comparison on page three of continued TPCC reporting on the Overseas Private Investment Corporation's budget and its cessation of reporting on U.S. Agency for International Development's (USAID's) budget. This commentary excludes the important fact discussed during our interviews and in supporting memoranda that USAID chose in 1999 to omit itself from the TPCC process. This fact is important as it emphasizes the lack of authority to require TPCC agencies to provide budget and resource allocation information, which may constrain the TPCC's ability to permanently assume greater budget resource oversight responsibility.

The analysis also does not address what impact this information had when provided in 1998, 1999, 2000, and 2002. It is difficult for the TPCC Secretariat to convince the TPCC agencies to sustain such an information sharing exercise without showing a demonstrable impact. GAO states that having high quality budget information is necessary for decision makers to make informed recommendations on allocation for federal resources. GAO notes that the TPCC did collect standardized information throughout much of the 1990's and that despite the TPCC's efforts this information was never used to make resource allocation decisions. It would be helpful if GAO would provide guidance regarding what information would be most relevant to and most likely to be used by decision makers.

The Office of Management and Budget (OMB) already has a process for collecting and analyzing crosscutting trade promotion budget data, including the authority to propose shifting resources between agencies (an authority the TPCC does not have). The President's Annual Budget informs congressional appropriators and authorizers of agencies' recommended trade promotion budgets.

An area where the TPCC has made tremendous progress since the launching of the National Export Initiative is in establishing crosscutting performance measures in support of NEI priorities as reported in the 2011 and 2012 National Export Strategies. It would be helpful if GAO's recommendations would include guidance on tying crosscutting performance measures to crosscutting resource allocations, including any best practices from other studies.

These concerns aside, we are committed to taking advantage of the GAO's concrete recommendations and constructive intentions for improving the crosscutting management and reporting of federal government trade promotion programs and priorities. The President's February 2012 Presidential Memorandum on Maximizing the Effectiveness of Federal Programs and Functions Supporting Trade and Investment directs the Export Promotion Cabinet, in consultation with the TPCC, to evaluate the allocation of resources, make recommendations to the Director of OMB, and propose a unified federal trade promotion budget is a tremendous opportunity. With this political mandate, we can rely on agencies' support in establishing a new TPCC Budget Working Group to act upon GAO's recommendations and establish (or reestablish) a robust TPCC role as called for in its mandate to "assess the appropriate levels and allocation of resources among agencies in support of the export promotion and export financing and provide recommendations to the President based on its assessment…"

As this new process unfolds, we look forward to the possibility of further consultations with the GAO team.

Sincerely,

Pat Kirwan, Director
Trade Promotion Coordinating
Committee Secretariat

Appendix III: GAO Contact and Staff Acknowledgments

GAO Contact	Kimberly Gianopoulos, (202) 512-8612, gianopoulosk@gao.gov
Staff Acknowledgments	In addition to the contact named above, Adam Cowles, Assistant Director; Michael McAtee, Analyst-in-Charge; Kara Marshall; and Karen Deans made key contributions to this report.

Related GAO Products

Export Promotion: Small Business Administration Needs to Improve Collaboration to Implement Its Expanded Role. GAO-13-217. Washington, D.C.: January 30, 2013.

National Export Initiative: U.S. and Foreign Commercial Service Should Improve Performance and Resource Allocation Management. GAO-11-909, Washington, D.C.: September 29, 2011.

International Trade: Effective Export Programs Can Help In Achieving U.S. Economic Goals. GAO-09-480T. Washington, D.C.: March 17, 2009.

Export Promotion: Trade Promotion Coordinating Committee's Role Remains Limited. GAO-06-660T. Washington, D.C.: April 26, 2006.

Export Promotion: Mixed Progress in Achieving a Governmentwide Strategy. GAO-02-850. Washington, D.C.: September 4, 2002.

Export Promotion: Federal Agencies' Activities and Resources in Fiscal Year 1999. GAO/NSIAD-00-118. Washington, D.C.: April 10, 2000.

Export Promotion: Issues for Assessing the Governmentwide Strategy. GAO/T-NSIAD-98-105. Washington, D.C.: February 26, 1998.

National Export Strategy. GAO/NSIAD-96-132R. Washington, D.C.: March 26, 1996.

Export Promotion: Governmentwide Plan Contributes to Improvements. GAO/T-GGD-94-35. Washington, D.C.: October 26, 1993.

Export Promotion: Initial Assessment of Governmentwide Strategic Plan. GAO/T-GGD-93-48. Washington, D.C.: September 29, 1993.

Export Promotion Strategic Plan: Will It Be a Vehicle for Change? GAO/T-GGD-93-43. Washington, D.C.: July 26, 1993.

Export Promotion: Governmentwide Strategy Needed for Federal Programs. GAO/T-GGD-93-7. Washington, D.C.: March 15, 1993.

Export Promotion: Federal Programs Lack Organizational and Funding Cohesiveness. GAO/NSIAD-92-49. Washington, D.C.: January 10, 1992.

Please Print on Recycled Paper.